Cool & Calm Coloring for

Illustrations by Eugénie Va

Creative
Coloring
and Dot-to-Dots

BARRON'S

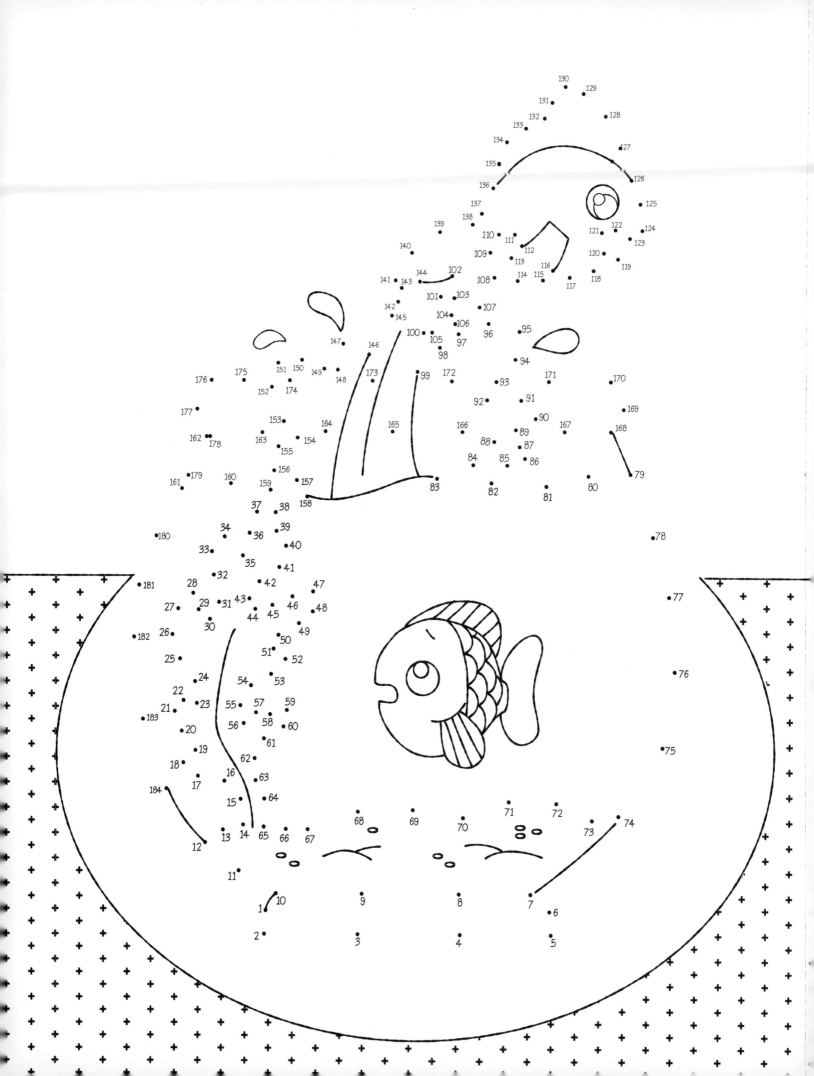

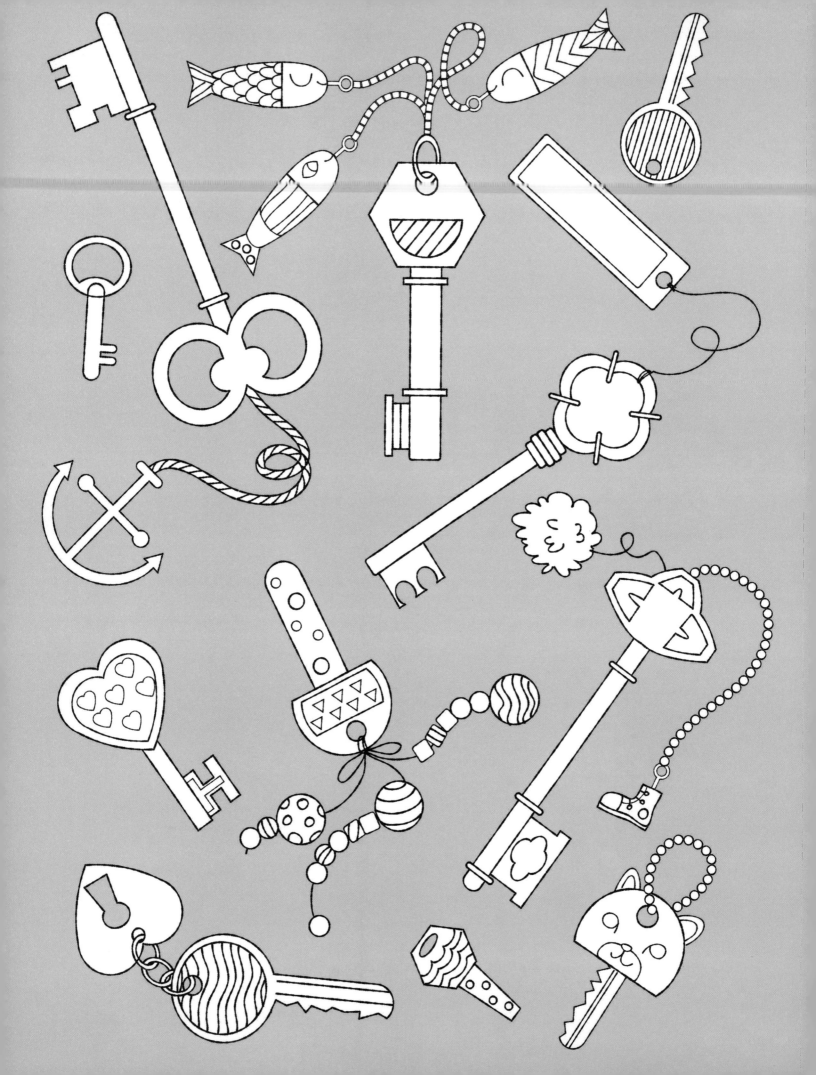

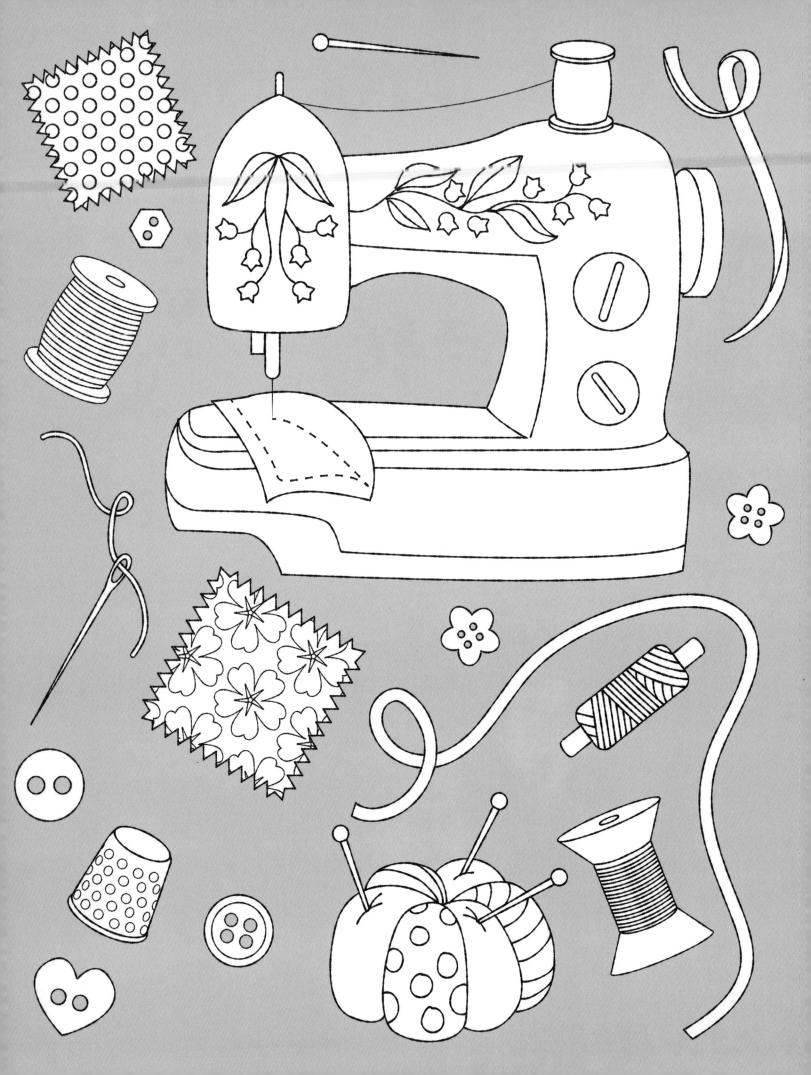

Published in the French language originally
under the title: **Coloriages et points à relier**
© 2015, Éditions Gründ, an imprint of Édi8, Paris

First edition for North America published in 2016 by Barron's Educational Series, Inc.

All inquiries should be addressed to:
Barron's Educational Series, Inc.
250 Wireless Boulevard
Hauppauge, New York 11788
www.barronseduc.com

ISBN: 978-1-4380-0883-7

Date of Manufacture: December 2015
Manufactured by: Leo Paper Group, Heshan, China

Printed in China

9 8 7 6 5 4 3 2 1